HISTORY RELIVED

The Romans

Cath Senker

Photographs by Martyn F. Chillmaid

WAYLAND

HISTORY RELIVED

This book is a differentiated text version of *The Romans* by Jason Hook.

Conceived and produced for Wayland by

Nutshell
MEDIA

www.nutshellmedialtd.co.uk

This edition first published in 2009 by Wayland.

© Copyright 2009 Nutshell Media Ltd

Editor: Polly Goodman
Original designer: Simon Borrough
Layout for this edition: Jane Hawkins
All reconstructions set up and photographed by: Martyn F. Chillmaid

British Library Cataloguing in Publication Data
Senker, Cath.
The Romans. -- Differentiated ed. -- (History relived)
1. Romans--Great Britain--Social life and customs--Juvenile literature.
2. Great Britain--History--Roman period, 55 B.C.-449 A.D.--Juvenile literature.
I. Title II. Series III. Hook, Jason. Romans reconstructed.
936.1'04-dc22

ISBN: 978 0 7502 5862 3

Printed and bound in China

Wayland is a division of Hachette Children's Books,
A Hachette UK Company

www.hachette.co.uk

Cover photographs: Top left: Roman soldiers stand outside the gates of a fort;
Centre left: soldiers join their shields together to make a shape known as the tortoise;
Bottom left: a slave brings in the first course of dinner;
Right: a father and his son wearing togas.

Title page: Drinking wine at the evening meal.

Contents

Roman Britain

In 43 CE, a Roman army invaded Britain. Emperor Claudius of Rome wanted to make Britain part of the Roman Empire.

The Roman army was divided into groups of 80 soldiers. Each group was called a century. The soldiers were called legionaries. Each century was led by a centurion. Soldiers called signifers carried the army's banners. Soldiers called cornicens blew horns to give signals.

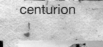

signifer   army banner   centurion

legionary   medals   cornicen

▼ Roman legionaries in Britain.

In Britain, people lived in tribes. They lived in settlements of small, round huts with thatched roofs. Around each settlement there was a ditch and a wooden fence. Sentries looked out for enemies from watchtowers.

roof made with straw

wooden fence

watchtower

▲ A settlement in Britain.

The Britons were fierce fighters. The tribes were used to fighting each other. But the Romans were better organized and they easily beat the Britons.

The Romans slowly took over England and Wales. They called their country Britannia. Over the next 350 years, the Romans built cities, villas, market places and hundreds of kilometres of roads.

Fighting

▲ Soldiers in the 'tortoise' shape.

The Roman legionaries had better equipment than their enemies and they had clever ways of fighting.

The soldiers had shields made of wood or leather. In battle, they joined the shields together to make a shape called the *testudo*, which means 'tortoise'. The *testudo* was very strong. It was said you could drive a chariot over it!

shield

gap to see out

iron stud

sandals

The legionaries wore armour to protect themselves. They wore helmets that covered their head, cheeks and neck. A studded apron protected their groin.

When they attacked their enemies, the Romans followed a careful plan. First, they fired giant crossbows. Sometimes they fired rocks with a big catapult.

Next they moved towards their enemies in the *testudo* shape. They spread out in a line and hurled javelins. Then they came up close. They hit their enemies with their shields, and stabbed them with their swords and daggers.

armour

helmet

tunic

dagger

sword

catapult

basket of rocks

lever

▼ Firing a catapult.

A Roman Fort

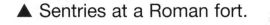

▲ Sentries at a Roman fort.

The Romans built forts to protect themselves from enemy British tribes. They lived inside the forts.

Roman forts had four walls. To build each wall, first the soldiers dug a ditch. Then they piled up the earth behind it to make a bank and covered the bank with grass. Along the top, they built wooden ramparts.

wooden ramparts   bank

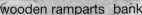

sentry   patrol

Along the top of the ramparts there was a path. From there, the sentries looked out for enemies. There was a gate on each side of the fort. Each gateway had a higher rampart above it. If enemies reached the gate, sentries threw missiles at them from the rampart above.

The inside of the fort was like a Roman town. There were streets laid out in a grid pattern, with buildings on each side. The blacksmith had a workshop where he mended wagons and carts. There was a hospital with a room for operations. A granary was built above the ground to keep grain dry and away from rats. Just outside the fort, there was a bathhouse.

The soldiers slept in barracks. A group of eight legionaries shared a room. A centurion had four rooms to himself. The commander, who ran the fort, had his own house.

▲ The gate of a fort.

sentry

gates

ladder to higher ramparts

Soldiers

When the Romans took over Britain, many Britons joined the Roman army. These soldiers were called auxiliaries.

The new soldiers practised fighting with wooden poles and wickerwork shields. Auxiliaries who served in the army for over 25 years became Roman citizens.

▼ Auxiliaries practise fighting.

legionary

wickerwork shield

sandals

auxiliary

woollen tunic

apron with studs

leather bag

flask

javelin

metal mess tin

Roman soldiers practised marching so that they could move faster and further than their enemies. Legionaries practised by marching 30 kilometres in five hours, carrying packs weighing 20 kilograms. They wore sandals with iron nails in the soles to make the sandals last longer.

A legionary carried his equipment over his shoulder, on a pole. He carried tools and wooden posts for making a camp, and a javelin. His leather bag held spare clothes. In cold northern Britain, legionaries wore heavy cloaks.

Legionaries also carried a flask of sour wine and a mess tin (pan) for meals. They ate bread, beans, onions, lentils and fish.

◀ A legionary's equipment.

Roads and Chariots

When the Romans arrived in Britain, there were no proper roads. So they began to build long, straight roads. Workers dug them out. Then they filled the roads with sand and stone.

▼ The Roman road at Blackstone Edge, Lancashire.

paving stones

kerb stones

gutter

Most Roman roads were covered with small stones. The road in the photo above is paved with bigger flat stones and has kerbstones. There is a gutter in the centre of the road. If a cart driver needed to stop, he pressed a pole into the gutter.

Traders, soldiers and messengers used the roads. Every Roman mile (1.4 kilometres) there was a stone post, called a milestone. The milestones showed the distance to the nearest city. About every 20 kilometres there was a post house, where messengers on horseback swapped tired horses for fresh ones.

spina

whip

chariot

wheel falling off

rider falling off

▲ Chariot racing, seen on a mosaic in Britain.

The Romans also used horses for chariot racing. In Rome, there was a huge racecourse called the Circus Maximus. In Britain, the Romans probably marked out quite basic tracks on areas of flat ground. The chariots raced around a long barrier, called the *spina*. There were many accidents!

Houses

Soon after they invaded Britain, the Romans built towns. The towns had well-planned streets, running water and sewers.

Rich families lived in large houses with five or six rooms. In the middle was a courtyard garden, called the *peristilium*. Here there were herbs, flowers and statues of gods.

statue   slave   pond   flowers   herbs

▼ A family in their garden.

▲ A slave builds a fire.

Many town houses had glass windows, painted walls and mosaic floors. There was an oven in the kitchen.

Rich families had many slaves. The slaves did all the housework. They cooked the food, cleaned the house and looked after the children.

Some slaves were treated well and became like members of the family. Other slaves were treated badly. If they did not do as they were told, they were beaten.

firewood   herbs

oven   earth floor

Mosaics

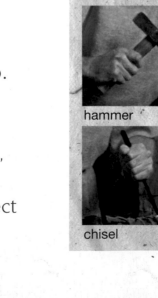

▲ A craftsman making a mosaic.

The Romans brought mosaics to Britain. At first, only Roman craftspeople could make them. Then Britons learnt the skills, too.

There were many kinds of stone in Britain – white chalk, grey limestone, yellow sandstone, red ironstone and black slate. These colours were perfect for making a mosaic.

tesserae   stone bench

hammer   saw

chisel   set squares

16

It took a long time and great skill to make a mosaic floor. Only the richest people could afford to have one made in their own house.

First, a skilled craftsman drew the design. Then mosaic workers cut up thousands of tiny stones, called *tesserae*.

At the house, the workers laid cement and scratched the design of the mosaic on the surface. Then they poured on a mixture of lime and water, and pressed the *tesserae* down. The workers used set squares to place the pieces neatly. Lastly, they polished the floor.

dividers

tesserae

chisels

mosaic

▼ A worker finishes a mosaic.

pincers

Hair and Clothes

The Romans liked to look their best –
especially the women.

Wealthy women pinned their hair up in plaits
and curls. Some wore wigs made from the hair
of their slave girls. They used chalk or white
lead to lighten their face and arms, and red
ochre to make their cheeks look brighter.

Women sometimes used face packs of bread
and milk to help them look younger. They
could even buy false teeth.

plait

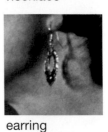
necklace

red ochre

earring

eyeshadow

painted ceiling

▼ A slave pins up her mistress's hair.

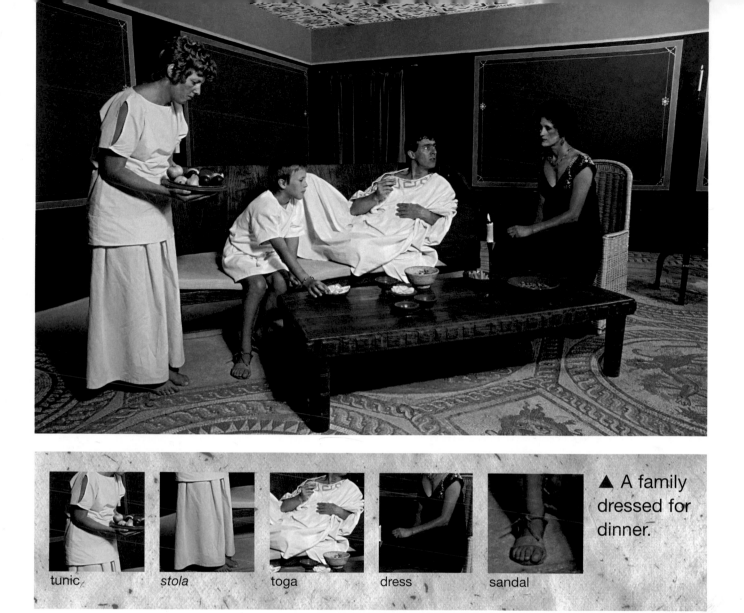

tunic   *stola*   toga   dress   sandal

▲ A family dressed for dinner.

Men wore tunics. Over the top they wrapped a big woollen cloth, called a toga.

Women wore a long tunic called a *stola*, with a shorter tunic on top. They used pretty brooches to fasten their clothes. Rich women wore necklaces and earrings made from gold, silver or glass. Cheaper jewellery was made from bone, glass or pottery.

At home, both men and women wore sandals. When they went out, they put on leather boots.

Children

Children were very precious to the Romans. Parents asked the household gods to protect them.

When a baby was nine days old, the parents gave him or her a locket, called a *bulla*. The locket held charms to keep the baby safe.

white toga

tunic

purple edge

sandal

In their homes, parents offered food to statues of the gods. Children did this, too.

▲ A father and son in their togas.

A Roman boy wore a toga with a purple edge. When he reached 16, he offered this toga and his *bulla* to the gods. He thanked the gods for letting him grow up to become a man. Then he put on a plain white adult toga.

From the age of seven, a boy learnt his father's work. Rich children also had slaves to teach them to read and write. They learnt to dance and play the *cithara*, an instrument like a harp. Some children went to school, which was often in the forum.

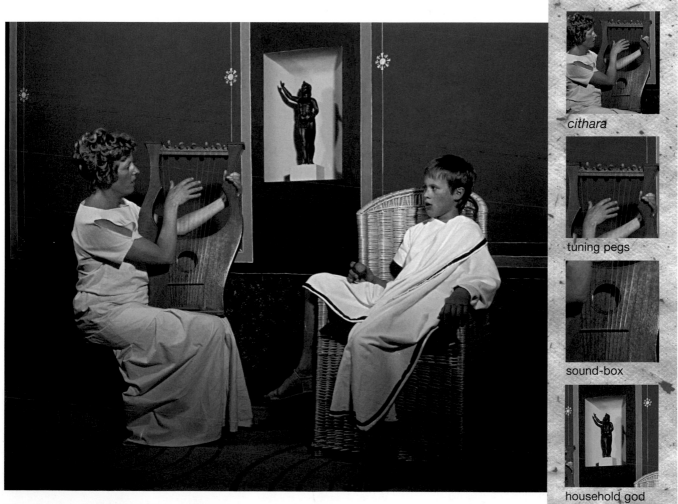

cithara

tuning pegs

sound-box

household god

▲ A slave plays the *cithara*.

In their free time, children played with rattles, dolls, hoops and swings. Some had toy chariots, which they tied to mice or birds.

Food

In a townhouse kitchen, slave cooks hung hares and pigeons on the walls. They kept spices in pots.

Slaves had many tools for preparing food. They used a cleaver to cut meat. A pestle and mortar were used for grinding spices. Pots of food were cooked on a grid-iron over a charcoal fire.

Many kitchen goods were bought from other countries. Pottery came from Gaul (France). Wine and olive oil came from Spain, Greece, Italy and Gaul. They were shipped in tall jars called *amphorae*.

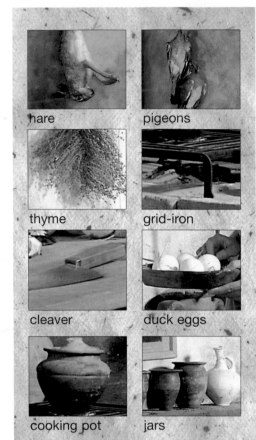

hare   pigeons

thyme   grid-iron

cleaver   duck eggs

cooking pot   jars

▼ A slave and her mistress in the kitchen.

▼ Roman herbs and spices.

ginger

garlic

rosemary

peppercorns

amphora

parsley

mint

onions

bay leaves

sage

Food did not always arrive fresh. Cooks used
sauces, herbs and spices to cover up the bad taste.
The Romans loved strong fish sauce made from
rotting fish guts and herbs!

The Romans used parsley, sage and other herbs.
Their favourite spice was pepper. Cooks added
peppercorns to sauces and even to desserts.

Roman Dinners

The Romans often invited friends for dinner. They ate on low couches, leaning on cushions stuffed with straw.

Roman diners used spoons and knives, but no forks. They mostly ate with their fingers, so dinner was very messy!

The Romans drank cheap wine mixed with honey or water. They often became drunk.

▼ Romans thought wearing rose petals would stop them feeling ill if they drank too much wine.

wine jar

candle

cup of wine

rose petals

▲ The first course.

For the first course, there were lots of small dishes such as snails, fruit, nuts and cucumber salad. There were hard-boiled eggs and beans with chickpeas.

For the main course, the Romans liked roasted peacock or boar, and dormice stuffed with pork. They ate peas, leeks, onions, and a new vegetable that the Romans brought to Britain – the turnip. If they had any room for dessert, there were light puddings such as honey cake.

cucumber salad

eggs

fruit

snails

beans with chickpeas

carrots

nuts

couch

Roman Baths

▲ A Roman bath.

The Romans built public baths all around Britain. They were a place to chat, play games, wash and relax.

The baths were huge buildings, with tall stone pillars and high ceilings. They were decorated with beautiful mosaics of gods and sea animals.

Women visited the baths in the morning. Men visited in the afternoon. They moved through several different rooms and baths during each visit.

The first bath was the warm *tepidarium*. Then there was the *caldarium*, with hot steam. Here, slaves rubbed oil into the bathers' skin. They scraped off the oil and dirt with a tool called a *strigil*. Afterwards, the bathers jumped into the freezing water of the *frigidarium*.

Many Roman inventions were used to build the baths. Channels called aqueducts carried water. Hot air was pumped under the floors to make them warm.

The remains of Roman inventions, such as the baths, mosaics and roads, all help us to learn about life in Roman Britain.

fire to heat floor

warm floor

tiles

▼ The floor was raised on tiles.
It was heated underneath.

Timeline

55 BCE and 54 BCE

The Roman general Julius Caesar tries to invade Britain, but fails both times.

43 CE

A Roman army invades Britain.

44 CE

Roman legionaries defeat Britons at Maiden Castle, in Dorset.

c. 50 CE

The Romans build towns in Britain. They include London, Dorchester, Chichester, Colchester and St Albans.

c. 60 CE

Britons fight against Roman rule. The Roman army defeats them.

c. 75 CE

The Romans start to build villas in Britain.

78 CE

The Romans take over Wales.

c. 80 CE

The Romans finish building a network of roads across Britain.

122 CE

The Romans start to build Hadrian's Wall in the north of Britain to protect themselves from Scottish tribes.

208 CE

Hadrian's Wall is broken. The Roman emperor Septimus Severus comes to Britain to fight tribes that are invading England from Scotland.

367–9 CE

Groups from Scotland, Ireland and Germany attack Roman Britain.

c. 400 CE

Many Roman troops leave Britain to help protect Rome.

By 410 CE

The Roman troops have left Britain. The end of Roman Britain.

Note

The letter 'c' is short for *circa*. When you are talking about dates, this means 'around'.

The letters BCE and CE refer to the Christian calendar. BCE stands for 'Before Common Era'. For Christians, this refers to the years before Christ was born.

CE is short for 'Common Era'. For Christians, this refers to the years after Christ was born. If something happened in 44 CE, it happened 44 years after Christ was born.

Glossary

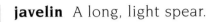

aqueduct A system of pipes that brings clean water into towns.

auxiliary Foreign soldiers who fought with the Roman army.

barracks Housing blocks for soldiers.

bathhouse A place with hot and cold baths where the Romans washed, swam and did exercises.

blacksmith A person who makes and mends things made of iron.

catapult A weapon for throwing heavy stones.

centurion An officer in the Roman army, in charge of a century.

charcoal A black substance made from wood that can be burnt as fuel.

chariot A two-wheeled cart pulled by horses.

charm A small object supposed to bring good luck.

citizen A person who has the right to belong to a country.

crossbow A bow fixed on to a piece of wood, used for shooting heavy arrows.

empire A group of countries that are ruled by a foreign country.

forum An open area in the middle of a Roman city where people gathered for meetings, shopping, games and religious events.

grid pattern A criss-cross pattern with straight lines going up and down, and from side to side.

javelin A long, light spear.

legionary A soldier in the Roman army.

locket A piece of jewellery that opens and can be used to store small objects such as photographs or locks of hair.

missile An object thrown at someone to hurt him or her.

mosaic A decoration made by placing tiny pieces of stone together.

ochre A kind of red earth.

pestle and mortar A tool and bowl used for grinding food.

ramparts The walls of a fort, with a path along the top.

running water Water that is brought to a building through pipes.

sentries Soldiers working as guards.

settlement A place where people live together, such as a village or a town.

set square A triangular tool used for measuring angles.

sewer A pipe under the ground to take away dirty water from buildings.

slave A person who is owned by another and is forced to work for him or her.

toga A loose piece of clothing worn by Roman men.

villa A large country house.

watchtower A high, safe place with a good view of the area. A guard watches out for enemies from the watchtower.

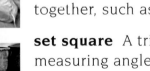

Activities

pp4–5 Roman Britain

- Use tracing paper to copy the picture on page 4. Label it with information about Roman soldiers' clothes and equipment.

- With other members of your class, imagine you are a Roman army about to invade Britain. Choose who is going to be the centurion, and who are going to be legionaries, signifers and cornicens. Write a short play about your invasion and act it out.

- Design and make your own banner for a century of your class.

pp6–7 Fighting

- Look at the photo on page 6 and use a large piece of card to make a model of a Roman shield. Paint your own war-like design on it. You can use a bottle top to make the stud in the middle.

- Use the Internet to find out how to make a simple catapult out of ice-lolly sticks and rubber bands.

- Write a list of instructions to explain how to fire a catapult.

pp8–9 A Roman Fort

- Use the information on pages 8–9 to draw a plan of a Roman fort. Show the walls, ramparts, gates, streets and different buildings on your plan.

- Imagine you are a Roman sentry on watch in a fort and you spot some enemies in the distance. In a role play with other members of your class, act out what you would do.

pp10–11 Soldiers

- Use the Internet to find maps of the Roman Empire. Draw and colour in your map to show the different countries ruled by Rome.

- Imagine you are a Roman legionary. Write a letter to your family in Rome.

pp12–13 Roads and Chariots

- Look at a modern road map. Can you spot the straight Roman roads?

- Make a chariot-racing board game using card. Make your own counters. Write down the rules of the game.

pp14–15 Houses

- Imagine that you are a Roman slave in a townhouse. Write a diary describing one day, listing all the jobs that you have done.

pp16–17 Mosaics

- Make your own mosaic using card in different colours. Cut up tiny pieces of card, then stick them on to a large piece of card to make a picture. You could copy a Roman design like the one on page 17.

pp18–19 Make-up and Fashion

- Draw a Roman family wearing all the clothes on page 19. Label the clothes in your drawing.

- Ask an adult to help you make a Roman toga from old white sheets.

pp20–21 Children

- Find out as much as you can about Roman toys, games and musical instruments. Compare them to the ones we have today.

- Find the Roman numbers from one to ten from a book or the Internet and practise writing them.

pp22–23 Food

- Ask an adult to help you find or buy some of the herbs and spices the Romans used.

- Think of a revolting Roman dish using some of the ingredients on page 22. Write a recipe for it.

pp24–25 Roman Dinners

- Write and draw your own menu for a Roman dinner party, with three courses.

pp26–27 Roman Baths

- Design a poster advertising some Roman public baths.

- Go to your local library or tourist information centre. Ask if there are any Roman buildings or ruins in your area. See if you can visit them.

- Find out about Roman inventions such as aqueducts, central heating, drains and concrete.

Find Out More

BOOKS TO READ

Find Out About Ancient Rome by Jane Bingham (Wayland, 2008)

The Gruesome Truth about the Romans by Jillian Powell (Wayland, 2008)

The History Detective Investigates Roman Britain by Peter Hepplewhite (Wayland, 2008)

Men, Women and Children in Ancient Rome by Jane Bingham (Wayland, 2007)

Roman Life: Homes by Paul Harrison (Wayland, 2009)

Roman Life: Work by Nicky Barber (Wayland, 2009)

The Romans in Britain by Robert Hull (Wayland, 2007)

PLACES TO VISIT

Corinium Museum, Gloucestershire
www.coriniummuseum.co.uk/
Many of the photographs in this book were taken at this museum.

The Ermine Street Guard, Gloucestershire
www.erminestreetguard.co.uk/
This organization gives displays of Roman soldiers and their equipment. Some of the photographs for this book were taken with the Guard's help.

The Roman Baths, Bath
www.romanbaths.co.uk/
You can visit the baths where the photograph on page 26 was taken.

Index

Page numbers in **bold** means there is a photo on the page.

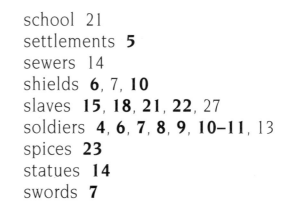

History Relived

Contents of titles in the series: